THE
PURR-FECT
LITTLE BOOK OF
CATS

THE PURR-FECT LITTLE BOOK OF CATS

Robyn Officer

Ariel Books

Andrews McMeel Publishing

Kansas City

THE PURR-FECT LITTLE BOOK OF
CATS

For information, write Andrews McMeel Publishing, an Andrews McMeel Universal company, 4520 Main Street, Kansas City, Missouri 64111.

www.andrewsmcmeel.com

ISBN: 0-8362-3604-1

Library of Congress Catalog Card Number: 97-74533

THE PURR-FECT LITTLE BOOK OF CATS

INTRODUCTION

Cats: What do they want? What are they thinking? Freud wouldn't know where to start. A cat curled on the hearth is the very picture of a cozy home, and her purr is the very sound of contentment. These creatures are beautiful at rest and

glamorous in motion; they
are formidable in battle and
boisterous in
love.

Throughout the ages cats
have been deified and reviled,
pampered and persecuted. And
still cats are not a neutral
subject: We either love them
or hate them. The dog is an

icon of unswerving loyalty; the cat, no matter how useful or affectionate, seems to have her own agenda. Even though she shows up to demand that tin of cat food every day, the cat is independent: She stays by choice. Perhaps that's the secret of her appeal.

Mewsings:

Quotes about

Cats

Cats are
      mysterious
beings. . . .
You never know if they
love you or if they
condescend to occupy
      your house.
This mystery is what
   makes them the

most attractive beast.

Paul Moore

KITTENS

can happen to anyone.

Paul Gallico

. . . Those dear, sweet, little lumps, stumping and padding about the house, pulling over electric lamps, making little puddles in slippers, crawling up my legs, onto my lap (my legs are scratched by them, like Lazarus's), I see myself finding a kitten in the sleeve when I'm putting on my coat, and my tie under the bed when I want to put it on. . . .

Karel Čapek

They sleep in the bed
and go in and out of the
cat door all night —
I shudder to think
what the laundry

thinks we do to our
sheets, because it's a
sea of mud
    some nights.
If they go in and out a
lot, all you get are
        little
        black
        pawprints.

Sian Phillips

Whenever the cat of the house is black, the lasses of lovers will have no lack.

Folk saying

It is bad luck to
see a white cat
at night.

American superstition

A Cat's a cat

Everything that moves, serves to interest and amuse a cat. He is convinced that nature is busying herself with his diversion; he can conceive of no other purpose in the universe.

F. A. Paradis De Moncrif

& that's that.

Folk saying

Cat Tales...

You don't need a pet psychiatrist to tell you how your cat is feeling — just watch your feline's tail. A tail held high means happiness; a twitching tail is a warning sign; and a tail tucked in close to the body is a sure sign of insecurity.

If a cat washes behind its ears, it will rain.

Superstition

A cat sleeping with all four paws tucked under means cold weather ahead.

Superstition

To err is human,
To purr, is feline.

Robert Byrne

Even if you have just destroyed a Ming vase, purr. Usually all will be forgiven.

Lenny Rubenstein

A cat can purr its way
out of anything.

Donna Mc Crohan

PURRR...

CAT KIN

Whimsical cat breeds

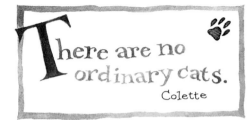

There are no
ordinary cats.

Colette

Hairless
SPHYNX

RUSSIAN
SHORTHAIR

AMERICAN
WIREHAIR

EGYPTIAN MAU

CALIFORNIA
SPANGLED

BRITISH
SHORTHAIR

SIAMESE

PERSIAN

RAG
DOLL

SCOTTISH FOLD

JAPANESE
BOBTAIL

SNOWSHOE

Exotic

TIFFANY

Catty-corner

Cat Nips

A silly selection of cat puns

Cat...

Cattails

CatMint

Catfish

Cool Cats

BobCat   TomCat

Cat Nap

Cat Call

Cat Gut

Cat-o'-nine-tails

Cat
Burglar

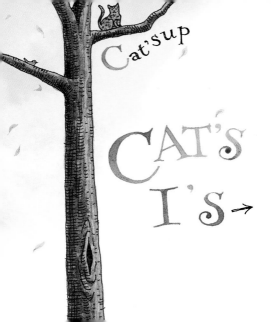

Cat'sup

CAT'S

I'S →

Catacomb

Catapult

CATAS

TROPHE!

MORE
Mewsings

Because his
long, white
whiskers
tickled, I began
every day
laughing.

Janet F. Faure

A

dog is a dog,
a bird
is a bird,
and
a cat is
a
person.

Mugsy Peabody

THE TROUBLE WITH CATS IS THAT THEY'VE GOT NO TACT.

P.G. Wodehouse

Cats have intercepted my footsteps at the ankle for so long that my gait, both at home

and on tour, has been compared to that of a man wading through low surf.

Roy Blount Jr.

N

o amount of time can erase the memory of a good cat, and no amount of masking tape can ever totally remove his fur from your couch.

LeoDworken

It's very hard to be

polite if you're a cat.

Anonymous

I don't mind a cat, in its place. But its place is not in the middle of my back at 4 A.M.

Maynard Good Stoddard

Most beds sleep up to
six cats.
Ten cats without the
owner.

Steven Baker

I soon realized
the name Pouncer
in no way
did

justice to her
aerial skills.
By the end of
the first
day

I had amended
her name to

KAMIKAZE.

Cleveland Amory

Oh cat, I'd say, or pray:
be-ootiful cat!

Delicious cat!
        Exquisite cat!
Satiny cat! Cat like a
soft owl, cat with paws
like moths, jeweled
        cat,
miraculous cat!

Cat,
cat, cat,
cat.

Doris Lessing